CHRONICLES

Searching for Sunken Treasure

Connery School
GRADE 4

By George Capaccio
Illustrated by Michael Italiaander

PUBLISHED BY THE NATIONAL GEOGRAPHIC SOCIETY

Produced through the worldwide resources of the National Geographic Society, John M. Fahey, Jr., President and Chief Executive Officer; Gilbert M. Grosvenor, Chairman of the Board.

PREPARED BY NATIONAL GEOGRAPHIC SCHOOL PUBLISHING

Sheron Long, Chief Executive Officer; Samuel Gesumaria, President; Francis Downey, Vice President and Publisher; Richard Easby, Editorial Manager; Anne M. Stone, Editor; Margaret Sidlosky, Director of Design and Illustrations; Jim Hiscott, Design Manager; Cynthia Olson, Ruth Ann Thompson, Art Directors; Matt Wascavage, Director of Publishing Services; Lisa Pergolizzi, Production Manager.

MANUFACTURING AND QUALITY CONTROL

Christopher A. Liedel, Chief Financial Officer; Phillip L. Schlosser, Vice President; Clifton M. Brown III, Director.

CONSULTANT

Mary Anne Wengel

BOOK DESIGN

Artful Doodlers and Insight Design Concepts Ltd.

Published by the National Geographic Society
1145 17th Street N.W.
Washington, D.C. 20036-4688

Product #4U1005087
ISBN: 978-1-4263-5080-1

Printed in Mexico

13
10 9 8 7 6 5 4 3

Contents

Searching for Treasure

Frank Starr drummed his fingers on the desk while his computer whirred to life. He was waiting to hear about an assignment for NATIONAL GEOGRAPHIC. Where would they send him this time? He had to be ready for anything.

One thing was certain: It would be an adventure. Maybe he could take his son with him—as long as there wasn't too much danger involved. Cody had always wanted to see what his father did for a living. The computer beeped at Frank. His assignment had arrived!

From: National Geographic Society
To: Frank Starr
Subject: Searching for Sunken Treasure

NATIONAL GEOGRAPHIC

Dear Frank:

We have a new assignment for you. We want you to travel to the Florida Keys. A team of researchers there has been searching for a sunken ship. It was called the *Santa Rosa*. It sank off the Keys in 1733. This could be an important discovery—and we want pictures!

You will travel with a team of marine archaeologists from Florida State University. The team plans to leave for the research site in a week's time. Contact the boat's captain, Bo Conway, for more details.

Sincerely,
NGS

Frank and Cody Starr

Frank is on assignment for NATIONAL GEOGRAPHIC magazine. His son, Cody, tags along for the adventure.

Bo and Chico Conway

Bo studies shipwrecks and believes they have important stories to tell. His son, Chico, enjoys diving in search of lost wrecks.

Lucille Cormac

Lucille is also interested in shipwrecks—but mostly for the fame and treasure they may bring.

Florida Keys

Frank logged on to the Internet. He needed to research the Florida Keys. Why would a ship have wrecked there?

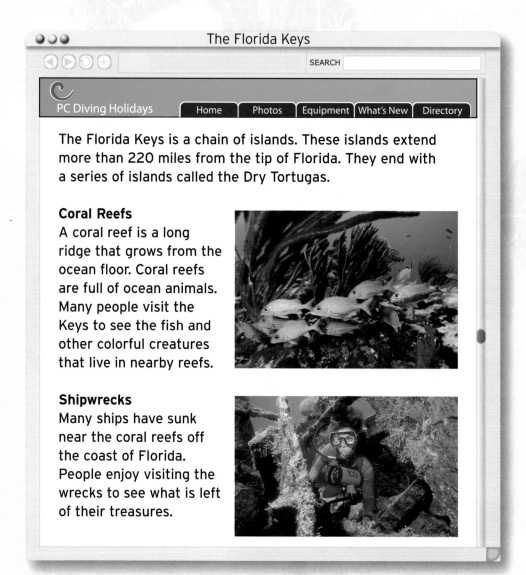

The Florida Keys

SEARCH

PC Diving Holidays | Home | Photos | Equipment | What's New | Directory

The Florida Keys is a chain of islands. These islands extend more than 220 miles from the tip of Florida. They end with a series of islands called the Dry Tortugas.

Coral Reefs
A coral reef is a long ridge that grows from the ocean floor. Coral reefs are full of ocean animals. Many people visit the Keys to see the fish and other colorful creatures that live in nearby reefs.

Shipwrecks
Many ships have sunk near the coral reefs off the coast of Florida. People enjoy visiting the wrecks to see what is left of their treasures.

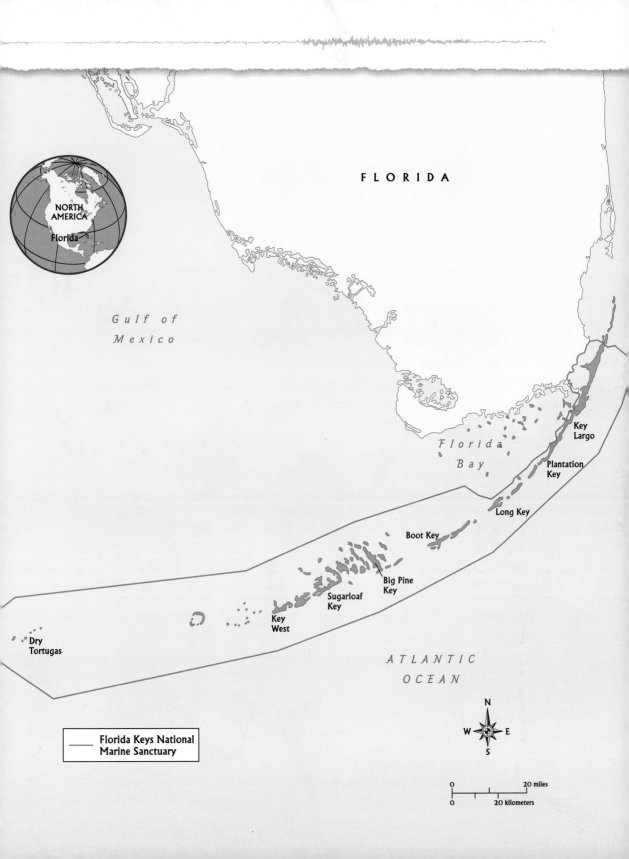

NORTH
AMERICA

Florida

FLORIDA

Gulf of
Mexico

Florida
Bay

Key
Largo

Plantation
Key

Long Key

Boot Key

Big Pine
Key

Sugarloaf
Key

Key
West

Dry
Tortugas

ATLANTIC
OCEAN

N
W E
S

Florida Keys National
Marine Sanctuary

0   20 miles

0   20 kilometers

CHAPTER 1

To Follow a Dream

The cab driver steered through the busy streets of Key West, Florida. His two passengers stared eagerly out the window.

"There's the marina!" Cody shouted as the cab rounded a corner. He had never seen so many boats in one place—sailboats, fishing boats, motorboats. One of them would soon take him on a voyage of discovery.

The cab parked near a waterfront restaurant. Cody jumped out. He couldn't wait to get started. Frank paid the driver, then checked the directions he had scribbled on a piece of paper.

"The pier we're looking for is over there," he said. He pointed toward a long wooden walkway with boats moored on either side.

Seagulls circled overhead. The wind carried the smell of salt water and engine fuel. As father and son neared the end of the pier, they heard the shrill sound of a whistle. They looked to see where it was coming from. Waving from the deck of his boat was a tall man. He wore khaki shorts, a bright yellow shirt, and a red baseball cap.

"Frank! Cody!" the man called out. "Welcome to the *Golden Pelican!*"

"You must be Captain Conway," Cody said.

"Call me Bo," the captain answered.

Cody spotted a boy about his own age on board the *Golden Pelican.* He was checking the gauges on an oxygen tank used for diving. "That's my son, Chico," the captain said.

"You and I will bunk together," Chico told Cody. "Grab your bags and follow me." He led Cody down a short ladder to a small room. It had two beds, one on top of the other, a chest of drawers, and a chair. There were no windows. Chico had already claimed the bottom bunk. Cody put his backpack on the top one.

"Have you ever hunted for sunken treasure before?" Chico asked.

"No, this is my first time. How about you?"

"I've done it lots of times. My dad's been taking me with him ever since I learned how to scuba dive. Check this out."

Chico took something shiny from his pocket and showed it to Cody. "It's called a gold doubloon," he said. "I found it in thirty feet of water near one of the reefs."

As Cody turned the coin over in his hand, he wondered about the weeks ahead. Would he actually find a sunken Spanish treasure ship?

Captain Conway poked his head in the room. "Would you like a tour of the boat?" he asked. Cody nodded, then flipped the gold coin in the air. Chico caught it in the palm of his hand. "See you later," he said as Cody left.

The *Golden Pelican* was not as small as Cody had thought it would be. It had a kitchen and dining room, three sleeping areas, and a large room that was used for meetings. Captain Conway took Frank and Cody in to meet the six-person research team. They were sitting at a table, studying a map.

"This is Sam Giancarlo," the captain said. "He's our team leader."

Sam shook hands with Frank and Cody. He looked younger than Cody's father and very fit. He had a dark moustache and deep-set eyes.

"I'm Mary, Sam's wife," said the woman beside him. She put down her glasses and smiled warmly. "We're both marine archaeologists from Florida State University. And these are some of our students: Ariana, Chris, Jennifer, and Jason. They are working with us on this trip."

Cody looked at the students. He guessed they were around twenty years old. They seemed very serious about their work.

Captain Conway sat down at the table. "So, Cody, have you had a chance to visit the websites I recommended?" the captain asked. Cody nodded.

"Great!" said the captain. "Can you tell me the purpose of our work?"

"We'll be searching the Florida Keys for a Spanish ship that sank during a hurricane in 1733," Cody began. "The ship's name was the *Santa Rosa*. It was part of a **fleet** carrying treasure to Spain."

----
fleet – a group of ships

"Excellent," the captain said. "And if we find the ship, then what do we do?"

Cody thought for a moment. "We try to learn as much as we can about her," he said.

Frank jumped in. "One way to do that is by studying her **artifacts,** the things the ship was carrying when she went down."

----
artifact – an object made by people long ago

"Like weapons, cannon, and things that belonged to the crew," said Ariana.

"Recovering artifacts from the ocean is very hard work," Jason said. "First we have to map the entire site and then decide which things to bring up and which to leave."

"Sometimes it's better to leave everything where it is," said Chris. "The main thing is to document as carefully as we can what's down there and where it was found. That way, other scientists will be able to continue our work."

The Florida Keys National Marine Sanctuary

There are many laws about diving for shipwrecks. That's because treasure hunters used to remove valuable artifacts and destroy wreck sites. Their equipment sometimes damaged the environment. In 1989 Florida set aside 2,800 square nautical miles of coastal waters as a National Marine Sanctuary. People can still visit this area. But treasure hunters must now apply for special licenses and agree to follow the rules.

"What about the treasure?" Cody asked.

Sam smiled. "We know the *Santa Rosa* was carrying a fortune in gold, silver, and precious stones," he said. "We think most of it is still with the ship. The rest was probably scattered across the ocean floor and may never be found."

"It would be great to find all that loot," said Mary as she drew a circle on the map in front of her. "But we would have to treat it as just another kind of artifact. We're marine archaeologists, not treasure hunters."

Cody had a new understanding of the work ahead of him. "So I guess the real treasure is what the ship can teach us about the past."

"Right!" said Bo.

Suddenly Chico bounded into the room. "Lucille Cormac's here!" he blurted out. "She's talking to some guy from Channel 7 News."

The captain scowled. "I wonder what she's up to this time," he said as they scrambled toward the deck.

"So who's Lucille Cormac?" Cody asked.

"That's her," said Bo gruffly. He pointed toward a woman with wild red hair, a bandanna around her neck, and silver bracelets on both wrists. She was sitting behind the wheel of her boat, the *Galleon Gold*. It was moored on the other side of the pier.

"She's a treasure hunter," the captain said. "I've got nothing against treasure hunters as long as they follow the rules. But Lucille is different. They say she's got pirate blood in her. I don't know if there's any truth in that, but I do know that when Lucille smells treasure, she stops at nothing to find it and claim it as her own."

A TV reporter was asking Lucille questions. A crowd of onlookers had gathered to listen. Bo, Frank, and Cody listened too.

"I've been searching for the *El Dorado* for a long time," Lucille said to the reporter. "She was

a treasure ship that sailed for Spain in 1733. She went down during a storm in the Keys. This time I know I'm going to find her."

"What makes you so sure?" the reporter asked.

"My crew has done some amazing research. All the latest signs point in one direction—the islands of the Dry Tortugas."

When the interview was over, Lucille spotted Bo. "Hey, Conway!" she yelled. "I hear you're on the trail of the *Santa Rosa*."

"That's right, Lucille."

"I bet I'll find my ship before you find yours."

Bo frowned and turned his back. Chico called from the front of the boat, "We're all set, Dad."

The captain went to the pilothouse. He stood behind the wheel and started up the engine. Then he took out the gold whistle he wore on a chain around his neck.

"Cody," he said, "this whistle is about 300 years old. I found it once while I was scuba diving." The captain blew a long, low note on the whistle. "When you hear that sound, it means we're leaving port." Cody watched as the marina slipped from view.

CHAPTER 2

The Storm

The next morning started out sunny. The ocean was calm. Cody leaned over one side of the boat. It was his first time on the open sea. He loved feeling the wind rush past him. He liked to imagine what lay hidden in the water below.

"It's time for school," he heard someone say. He looked up and saw Mary standing beside him.

"But I finished school last week," Cody said. "I've got the whole summer off."

"I know, but the captain wants to be sure you can handle yourself in the water. So he asked me to give you scuba diving lessons."

Cody couldn't believe his luck!

"You'll need to practice in shallow water before you can join the dive teams," Mary continued. "But if you're a fast learner and you follow the rules, you should be ready for your first dive by next week. Today I want to see how well you can swim with flippers and a face mask."

Mary went in first. Then it was Cody's turn. He climbed down a rope ladder and let himself fall backward into the ocean. The water was warm and only about six or seven feet deep.

Cody saw sea fans swaying in the current and schools of brightly colored fish. As he swam over a large piece of coral, he spotted a moray eel. It looked scary and mean. Cody kept his distance. Then he saw a long narrow fish with a mouthful of razor-sharp teeth. It had to be a barracuda!

Cody started to panic. What if the barracuda attacked? He began to flail. He looked at Mary. She pointed toward the surface. Cody knew what that meant: His first lesson was over. It was time to return to the boat.

"There's a storm coming," Chico said as
he helped Cody back on board. "My dad thinks
it could be a big one." A cloud covered the sun.
The sea looked gloomy.

Bo and Sam came down from the pilothouse.
They joined the others. "Mary, it doesn't look
good," said Bo. "I think we need to find shelter
from the weather."

"Where's the nearest port?" Mary asked.

"About 15 miles due east there's a small
island. We can drop anchor in the harbor and
spend the night there. Agreed?"

"Agreed," Mary and Sam replied. As Bo
changed course, the wind picked up speed.
Rain began to fall. Cody felt the boat roll with
the waves. "Dad, I think I'm going to be sick,"
he said, looking around for a bucket.

"Go below and lie down," his father said. "The lower you are in a boat, the less you feel its motion." Frank put on his yellow raincoat. He loved rough weather and had been through many storms in his life. Camera in hand, he tried to capture the feel of this one.

Weather in the Florida Keys

The weather can get really wild in the Florida Keys. Hurricanes are some of the most powerful storms down here. They bring thunderstorms, rain, and powerful winds. The winds can reach speeds of more than 100 miles per hour. There isn't much a boat can do against them! Hurricane season lasts six months, from June until November. Some of the worst storms happen in late summer.

By the time the *Golden Pelican* reached the island, the storm was in full force. It kept up through the rest of the afternoon and long into the evening.

Over dinner, Captain Conway talked about some of the storms he had experienced. "The Florida Keys is no place for beginners," he said. "There's no telling what the weather will do."

Sam nodded. "The Keys are unique," he said. "With their coral reefs and shallow waters, they're very dangerous. During hurricane season, lots of ships have blown off course. They often crash against the reefs or get stuck in the sandbars."

"I know," said Cody. "That's what happened to the *Santa Rosa*. A hurricane caught her and most of the fleet. The wind blew from the south and pushed the ships toward the reefs."

The conversation went on long after dinner. So did the storm. That night, in his bunk bed, Cody felt the boat rocking wildly from side to side. He was glad they were spending the night in a safe harbor and not on the open ocean. But there would be other nights, he thought, when their boat would be far from shore.

Chico was already sound asleep in the lower bunk. Cody tossed and turned. He kept thinking about storms at sea and Spanish **galleons.** He pictured them going down under giant waves. He hoped nothing like that would happen to the *Golden Pelican*.

---

galleon – a Spanish ship with square sails used from the 1400s to the 1700s

CHAPTER 3

Man Overboard!

Early the next day, Captain Conway blew a long, low note on his whistle. Cody knew what the sound meant. The *Golden Pelican* was leaving port.

Another boat, still anchored in the harbor, suddenly blew its horn.

"I should have guessed she'd be here!" the boys heard Bo shout.

"Who's he talking about?" Cody asked.

"It must be Lucille," Chico said.

The boys finished dressing and then went up on deck. Chico was right. Lucille must have slipped into the harbor during the night. She was having coffee on the *Galleon Gold,* moored not far away.

"Hey, Conway!" she yelled. "Found any treasure yet?"

"I wouldn't tell you if I had!" Bo shouted back.

"You and I don't agree on a lot of things," said Lucille. "But I respect you, Conway. That's why I'm prepared to make you a deal."

Bo tried to ignore her. He checked the fuel line one more time and then started the engine. It sprang straight to life.

"Come with my crew," Lucille shouted through cupped hands. "When we locate the *El Dorado,* it'll be the biggest find in years. We'll be rich. What do you say? Are you with me?"

"No way, Lucille," Bo answered. He raised the anchor and steered his boat out of the harbor. Soon they were back on the open sea.

The rest of the morning passed quietly. Cody's father loaded his latest photos into his computer. Sam studied a large navigation chart. Mary gave Cody his second lesson in scuba diving. This time she taught him how to clear his face mask, how to attach weights to his diving suit, and how to hook up his air tank.

Close to noon, Bo pointed toward something in the distance. "There she is!" he called out. Cody almost expected to see the *Santa Rosa* with the wind filling her sails. Instead he saw a small island.

"That is where we're headed," Sam said. He put his finger on the chart. "There's a coral reef about 2,000 feet from the shoreline of the island. Mary and I think the *Santa Rosa* broke up on that reef. If we're right, then the remains should be somewhere near here."

"And whatever she was carrying is probably scattered across the ocean floor," Cody added.

"Exactly," said Sam. "Do you know what a debris field is?" he asked.

Cody didn't hesitate. He had read about debris fields when he was getting ready for the trip.

"That's easy," he said. "When a ship sinks, it leaves behind a trail of stuff. Ships like the *Santa Rosa* often left anchors, wooden planks, cannon, and treasure."

"Plus bottles, swords, and other neat stuff," said Chico, sitting down beside Cody.

"Of course, many things wouldn't have lasted this long," Sam said. "But things made of iron, bronze, gold, or silver will last a very long time."

Sam and Mary gathered the team around the table. Chico, Cody, and his father joined them. Sam drew a box on the navigation chart. "We'll start here," he said.

"Last summer we searched in the same area," Mary added. "We found several artifacts that definitely belonged to the *Santa Rosa.*" She marked the spots where each of the artifacts had been found. Then she drew a line that connected the spots.

"The line points toward the reef," Sam said. "My bet is that we'll find the *Santa Rosa* in shallow water close to the reef."

Cody studied the marks that Mary had drawn on the chart. The others worked on getting their search tools ready. As they worked, they told Cody about their tools.

Search Tools

A magnetometer is a search tool. It detects objects made of metal. When it senses something made of iron, it sends out a strong electrical signal. The computer picks it up. The signal is called a "hit."

Side-scan sonar is another tool. It uses sound waves. These bounce off objects underwater. The signal that comes back makes an image on a video monitor.

Ariana lowered a magnetometer into the water. Cody sat in front of her laptop and watched the screen for signs of a hit. He didn't have long to wait. "We've got something!" he shouted. "It's right below us!"

"I'll find it!" someone called out.

"Chico!" Cody shouted as his friend dove over the side of the boat.

"What's the matter with that kid?" asked the captain. "Who gave him permission to dive?"

Bo cut the engine. He didn't want to risk an accident. The propeller blades could easily cut off a person's arm or leg. Frank took photos of the team as they went into action. Mary put on her face mask and fins. She was the best diver on the team. She had to be ready in case there was a problem. A minute passed. There was still no sign of Chico. Then another minute went by.

Cody spotted something moving through the water. His eyes widened in fear. Mary saw it too. "Bo!" she shouted. "There's a shark out there. By the size of his fin, I'd say he's pretty big."

"I'm going in," said Bo.

Just then, Chico popped up. He was out of breath but looking very much alive.

"Hey, everybody!" he shouted. "I must have gone down 20 feet. All I found was a metal trap."

"Chico, get out of the water right now," his father said as calmly as he could. Chico didn't know about the shark. It started swimming toward him. Then he saw it and started to panic. The rope ladder was still several yards away.

In a split second, Bo was hanging off the ladder with one hand. He thrust out his other hand to Chico. The boy grabbed it. Bo yanked his son right out of the water. For a moment, no one spoke. Chico was safe.

Then Chico's father began to yell. "You broke every rule in the book!" he scolded. "Nobody on this boat ever dives alone or without the proper gear! You got that, young man?"

"Yes, sir," said Chico as he climbed back on board the boat.

Captain Conway put his arms around his son. "Promise me you'll never do anything like that again," he said.

"I promise, Dad."

He pointed his camera at Ariana's hands. She fanned away some more sand from the stones, and then she saw them. Frank saw them too. So did Cody and Chico.

There was no mistaking what Ariana had uncovered: dozens of silver coins. Snap! Frank clicked the shutter.

When Sam Giancarlo went down for a look, he found numbers inscribed on the cannon. Later, on deck, he checked them against a list of cannon from the *Santa Rosa.* Much to his surprise, he found the same numbers on the list.

"Good news, folks!" he shouted. "The cannon came from the *Santa Rosa.* We're close! We're very close!"

At the end of the day, Bo cooked up a steaming pot of seafood chowder. It was time to kick back and celebrate.

After dinner, everyone sat outside. There was no moon, but the stars were so big and bright they looked like precious jewels. Bo pulled up a chair and looked around the circle of faces. The group had begun to feel like a family to him.

"Hey, Bo, how about a story," Mary said.

"A story, huh? Well, let's see. Has anybody ever heard 'The Curse of Mad Molly?'"

Nobody had, so Bo sat back in his chair and began the story.

"Hundreds of years ago there lived an Irish lady named Molly O'Hara. She came from a good family. Her husband was an officer in the British navy. But one day the Spanish accused her husband of piracy. They captured his ship and hung him from the main mast. When Molly heard what had happened, she nearly lost her mind. All she wanted was revenge. So she sailed to the Florida Keys and became a pirate."

Bo suddenly stopped his story. "I don't believe it!" he said. "She's here."

"Who?" Chico asked. "Mad Molly?"

"No, it's Lucille Cormac," Bo answered. "She followed us. That's her boat over there." He pointed toward a twinkling red light in the distance.

"How can you be sure?" Cody asked.

"I know Lucille. I know how she operates. That's her, all right. She smells treasure. If we do find the *Santa Rosa,* we had better make sure Lucille isn't anywhere around."

Bo leaned back in his chair and went on with his story.

"There never was a pirate like Mad Molly. She only attacked Spanish treasure ships, and she never lost a fight. But one day she got herself caught. They hung her from a tree on that very island over there. People say her treasure is buried there. But wouldn't you know it, Molly put a curse on the island before she died. The curse protects the loot. You better hope you never find it—because if you do, you won't live to tell the tale."

That night Cody dreamed that he and Chico had found an old treasure map. It led them along the beach and into a cavern. They discovered a pile of old bones there. The bones marked the spot where the treasure chest was buried. Just when they had dug it up, the tide came in. Wave after wave roared through the cavern. The boys had to find a way out or they would drown!

Chico spotted an opening. He grabbed Cody's arm, and the two boys ran for their lives—but they had gone only a few steps when they froze in their tracks. Someone was coming toward them. They saw her shadow on the wall. "This is my treasure, boys," they heard her say. "And you'll not have it." They saw her face.

Cody woke up screaming her name: "Mad Molly! Mad Molly!"

CHAPTER 5

Uncovering the Past

During breakfast the next morning, Sam made an announcement. "We're going to start mapping today. Do you boys want to help?" Chico and Cody nodded.

Mary stirred the honey in her tea. Then she said, "Before we can excavate an underwater site, we have to know how big it is and what it contains. We also have to know where everything is located."

"That's why we use a grid," said Cody.

"Right," said Mary. She drew a grid on her napkin and held it up for everyone to see. "The grids we use are made of plastic. Each one is divided into squares."

"So the first thing we have to do is place a grid over the entire site," Chico said.

"Right again! But that's only the beginning of the process," said Sam. "We can't write on the grid. So how do you think we keep track of where each artifact is located?"

Cody thought back to what he had learned about graphs and how every graph has an x and a y axis. "We could give a different letter to each of the bars going up or down, and a different number to each of the bars going across."

"That way, each square would have its own number and letter," said Chico. "Like A1 or C6."

"You boys catch on fast," said Mary. "Suppose we find a silver bowl in the C6 square of our grid. We write this information on underwater slates and then put it into our **logbook** later on. Plus, we photograph each square. As archaeologists, we want to see the big picture. If we know where the artifacts are in relation to each other, then we might be able to understand what happened."

When breakfast was over, Sam split the group into two teams. Cody, Chris, and Ariana made up one team. Chico, Jennifer, and Jason were on the other team. Cody's team went in first. Chris and Ariana set the grid in place. Then Cody helped them look for artifacts.

----

logbook – a book for recording important details and discoveries

It took most of the morning to map the site. After lunch, Sam decided it was time to start bringing up some of the artifacts. Each diver had a slate, a pencil, and a goodie bag. The goodie bags were for holding artifacts.

During his first dive of the afternoon, Chico found several silver coins. He also found some cannonballs and an old sword. Jennifer signed to him that he could put the coins in his goodie bag. He left the other artifacts right where they were.

Cody's team made the last dive of the day. Toward the end of the dive, he saw something flash. He brushed away some loose sand. There were three shiny gold coins. They had rested on the ocean floor for centuries. Yet they were as bright as the day they were made.

Frank swam over and took a picture of his son pointing proudly toward the coins. Then Chris gave him a "thumbs up." Cody put the coins in his goodie bag and swam toward the surface.

Both dive teams worked hard for the next two days. By the time they finished, they had brought up many artifacts. Most of them were made of metal. There were also some porcelain cups and bowls. Each diver put the contents of his goodie bag into a tank of salt water. The water kept the artifacts from falling apart. The divers also used their logbooks to record what they had found and where they had found it.

Still, no one had spotted the *Santa Rosa*. The boat's search tools picked up other hits in the search area. But none of them turned out to be the ship or its stash of treasure. By the end of the second week, everyone was starting to feel quite discouraged.

On Friday morning, Sam called a meeting. He tacked the chart to the wall. Red marks showed all the sites they had searched. Black marks showed where the most important artifacts had been found. "I still think we're on the right track," he said to the team. "I've asked Bo to take us closer to the reef. That's where we'll find the *Santa Rosa*—in shallow water."

Once again Cody studied the scatter pattern of the artifacts. Sam and Mary saw a straight line pointing toward the reef. But Cody saw something else.

"What if another storm pushed the *Santa Rosa* off the reef?" he asked.

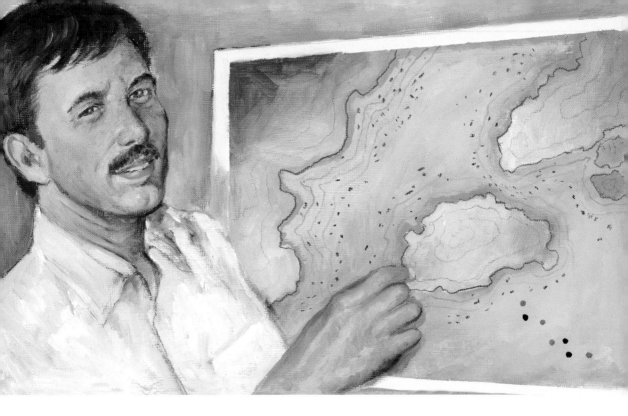

Chico's eyes lit up. "Right! And what if the ocean tide and the underwater currents carried her out to sea?"

Sam and Mary looked at each other. "You two might be on to something," Sam said. He went back to the chart on the wall. "If you're right, then the *Santa Rosa* could be here." Sam put his finger on a deep-water area. It was about half a mile from where they were now.

The room buzzed with excitement. Everyone was talking about the boys' new idea. Only Frank was quiet. He was proud of Cody. All he could do was smile.

CHAPTER 6

Rainbow's End

That same day, Captain Conway charted a new course to deeper water. It didn't take very long to get there. Then Bo set up a search pattern, and the team went to work with sonar. Soon the sonar showed a very large object in fifty feet of water. The team didn't know what it was. But they were determined to find out.

Jennifer and Jason went in first. When they surfaced, both were out of breath. "There's something down there!" Jason blurted out. "But we can't see it. The water is too murky." Sam asked Bo to use the mailbox. Ten minutes later, Jennifer broke the surface. "It's a ship's anchor. It must be about 15 feet long and probably weighs a ton."

Finding the anchor was a very good sign. Sam began to think that maybe the boys were right. Maybe the *Santa Rosa* was in deep water. There was only one way to find out—keep on searching.

The second dive team took over. Throughout the day, both dive teams had good luck. They found another anchor, more cannon, some cannonballs, and a long gold chain. Sam rubbed his hands together when he heard the good news. "Things are looking up. Things are definitely looking up," he said. "Today could be the day."

Cody set up his computer. He wanted to write about coral reefs. But as he started to type, he heard a strange sound. He looked up and saw a helicopter. It was hovering in place about 400 yards away. Right below it, the boys spotted a familiar boat. "Lucille!" they cried out together. Bo came up behind them and put his hands on their shoulders. "That's her, all right," he said. "I wonder what she's up to."

Bo didn't have to wait long. About a dozen other boats soon surrounded the *Galleon Gold*. Bo looked at them through a pair of binoculars.

"It appears that Lucille is about to make headlines," he said. "Every TV and radio news crew in the Keys is out there." Bo put down his binoculars. He marched back to the pilothouse. The entire team followed him. Everyone wanted to know why the newspeople had shown up.

Bo switched on the TV and tuned in a local station. "With me today is Lucille Cormac, a professional treasure hunter," the reporter said. "We're on her boat the *Galleon Gold*. Lucille, a few weeks ago you held a news conference in Key West. You announced the start of your latest search for the *El Dorado,* a Spanish treasure ship. Earlier today you reported a major find. Tell us more about it."

Bo and the rest of the team huddled around the TV. They didn't want to miss a single word.

"My crew and I have found a stunning collection of artifacts," Lucille said. "We believe

they come from the *El Dorado*. The ship sank in these waters more than 200 years ago."

"What exactly did you find?"

"Over 2,000 gold coins," Lucille answered. Then Lucille stared straight into the camera. She could barely contain her smile. "Bo, if you're watching, I have just one thing to say. Success comes to those who want it. I guess you don't want it badly enough."

Bo Conway snapped off the TV. "Back to work," he said. "We've got a ship to find."

Sam led the next dive team. The water was too deep for young divers like Cody and Chico. Cody went back to his computer, while Chico finished writing his notes in the logbook.

Twenty minutes later, Ariana broke the surface. "Folks, our search is over!" Then Sam popped his head up. "It's her all right—the *Santa Rosa!* And there's treasure everywhere!"

Bo let out a cheer. He tossed his baseball cap in the air. Then he blew his whistle as loudly as he could. Frank took pictures. He wanted to capture the looks of joy on people's faces. Jennifer put on her favorite CD and danced with Chris.

Bo stuffed a red flare in the flare gun and shot it straight up. It burst overhead and caught the attention of the newspeople. They were still interviewing Lucille Cormac.

Then Bo got on the ship-to-shore radio. He had some news of his own to share.

"This is Bo Conway, captain of the *Golden Pelican*. Our research team has just discovered the wreck of the *Santa Rosa*. It lies in 50 feet of water off the Dry Tortugas. Our divers report finding the remains of the ship's hull. And Lucille, if you're listening, we found treasure too. There are thousands of solid gold and silver bars, boxes of gold coins, jewelry made with emeralds and rubies. There must be over 500 million dollars' worth of treasure down there. But the real treasure, like I always say, is what we'll learn about the past."

Bo's announcement traveled fast. In less than a minute, it reached the news teams interviewing Lucille Cormac. The helicopter turned around and settled itself over the *Golden Pelican*. Lucille could only watch as the reporters and camera crews left her behind. They knew where the real scoop was.

Things soon returned to normal aboard the *Golden Pelican*. Now that the voyage was coming to an end, Frank Starr had an idea for one more photo. He asked Bo to stand with Cody and Chico in front of the pilothouse. Bo held up his golden whistle. The boys each held a golden coin. Everybody smiled. Frank took the picture.

Prepare for a Television Interview

The television news wants your opinion. Why is hunting for sunken ships important? Write a paragraph summarizing what you think.

- Copy the Venn diagram below.
- Use the diagram to show what Bo and Lucille think about searching for shipwrecks. How are their views similar? How are they different?
- Research at the library or online. What do other people think about searching for shipwrecks?
- Then write a paragraph explaining why it is important to hunt for sunken ships.

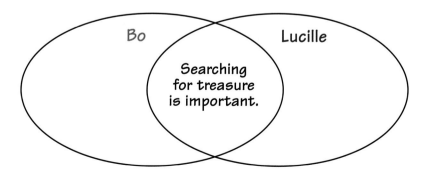

Bo   Lucille

Searching
for treasure
is important.

Read More About Shipwrecks

Find and read more books about shipwrecks. As you read, think about the following questions. They will help you understand more about this topic.

- Where can shipwrecks be found?
- What tools do scientists use to find shipwrecks?
- How do scientists preserve ships and artifacts that they discover?
- What can shipwrecks tell us about the past?

SUGGESTED READING
Reading Expeditions
Scientists in the Field
Discovering Underwater Treasures

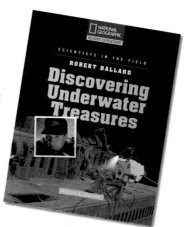